Rock and Pop SuperStars

Produced by
TED SMART and DAVID GIBBON

CRESCENT BOOKS

In the vanguard of a long line of rock 'n' rollers, **Johnnie Burnett** (1) was the heart-throb of millions.

A British group **The Tornadoes** (2) who translated the traditions of American rock 'n' roll to the British new-wave, with the sounds of electric guitars, clean-cut college boy looks and matching satin jackets!

Launching pad for the legendary Eric Clapton, the **Yardbirds** (3) were the prototype of many guitar-dominated sounds to come.

Peter Townshend (4) guitar – **Townshend and Roger Daltrey** (5) vocals – and **Daltrey** (6). Together with John Entwhistle

1

2

(bass) these two formed the original band, known as the Detours. Drummer Keith Moon joined them later, they changed their name to 'The Who' and built up a following whilst playing gigs in pubs in the Shepherds Bush area in the early Sixties.

In 1965 The Who reached No.2 with "My Generation," later to become a set-piece of their stage act. Their notorious auto-destructive act placed them heavily in debt, and The Who were not to begin making money until 1969 by which time they were a top live attraction on both sides of the Atlantic.

Success has followed, with many album releases, such as "Quadrophenia" and the highly-acclaimed rock opera "Tommy." Following the death of Keith Moon in September 1978, The Who have continued to make live appearances with his replacement, Kenny Jones.

3

4

5

6

1 & 2

1. **Peter Townshend** (The Who).
2. **Roger Daltrey and Keith Moon**
3 & 6. **Jerry Lee Lewis**

The Average White Band (4, 5 & 7) are as humorous as their name suggests. Possibly the closest a British band has come to producing real soul music! Formed in Scotland in early 1972 their first break was as support band to Eric Clapton, at his come-back gig at the London Rainbow in 1973. Since then, Average White Band have

5

7

switched their attentions primarily towards the United States market.

Britain's premier guitar hero, **Eric Clapton** (9) played with the Yardbirds, John Mayall, the Cream, John Lennon, Steve Stills and many others, before almost succumbing to depression and heroin addiction. Overcoming all these problems, Clapton made a successful comeback and has enjoyed ten years of uninterrupted success.

After breaking away from the highly successful Tamla Motown group; the Supremes, the lovely **Diana Ross** (8) has certainly come a long way from the Detroit ghetto where she was born. With more than sixteen No.1 hits to her credit, she is one of the most professional and charismatic all-round performers of our time.

8

Treading a path somewhere between straight showbiz, jazz and rock, **Elkie Brooks** (1, 2, 5) took eighteen years to gain her first solo hit "Pearl's A Singer" in the summer of 1977. Born in Lancashire, Elkie is now a regular T.V. guest and bill-topper. Although raunchy enough to satisfy rock audiences, she has a wistful way with a ballad - "Lilac Wine," "Gasoline Alley" – which ensures her allegiance

from many Middle-of-the-Road fans.

Cilla Black (4): this red-haired Liverpool lass of the Beatles generation has gone on to become a much-loved and lasting showbiz personality.

The American band "Blondie" owe much of their success in the late seventies to the striking sexuality and punk-chic style of lead singer **Deborah Harry** (6, 7, 8, 9). Blondie had enormous success with "Denis, Denis," and "Sunday Girl."

9

7

8

This US group **Bread** (1) started out as a soft-rock studio band who discovered that reaction to their records was so good that they had to equip themselves for concert appearances!

Guitarist and vocalist for one of Britain's most consistently entertaining singles groups since the mid-sixties, **Eric Stewart** (3) in fact played with songwriter Graham Gouldman in the original Mindbenders.

Born in Glasgow's notorious slum district, the Gorbals, in 1935, the late Alex Harvey was one of the few genuine characters of the U.K. rock scene. **The Sensational Alex Harvey Band** (2, 4, 5, 8) with its distinctive rock/theatrical style, was not formed until 1972 when it developed from other musical

combinations involving Alex Harvey.

The Searchers (6) recently celebrated twenty-one years in show business at their sell-out concert.

Foremost architects of the British "techno-rock" school, **Emerson, Lake & Palmer** (7) made their debut at the Isle of Wight Festival in 1970.

Four of the many faces of America's greatest ever rock 'n' roll star – the King – **Elvis Presley** (9-12).

9

10

11

12

The hard-rock/heavy metal band Queen (Freddie Mercury – vocals, Brian May – guitar, John Deacon – bass, Roger Taylor – drums) emerged during the early seventies to fill the gap left by Led Zeppelin's period of inactivity. After making the music for the children's adventure film "Flash Gordon," Queen had a monster hit with their single "Flash" and continue to maintain a prolific

The androgynous **Freddie Mercury** (1, 8), vocalist for Queen.

Billy Fury (2), successful pop idol of the sixties, made his comeback nearly twenty years later (3) only to die tragically at the age of 42 from a heart attack in January 1983.

The Hollies (4, 6) (Allan Clarke – vocals, Tony Hicks – guitar, Graham Nash – guitar, Bobby Elliott – drums). Originally formed in Manchester in 1963 at the beginning of the beat boom, the Hollies became Britain's most consistently successful chart act after the Beatles. From 1963-1970 they had an unbroken sequence of 21 Top Twenty hits.

Roger Taylor (5) the drummer with Queen. His solo album "Fun in Space" was released in 1980 and achieved some measure of success.

6

5

9

Yet another British rock group – **Deep Purple** (7) – (formed February 1968) that initially had greater success on the other side of the Atlantic. In 1970/71 their singles "Black Night" and "Strange Kind of Woman" did well in the UK where they worked hard to attain a heavier rock image. In 1976 guitarist Tommy Bolin died suddenly in Miami.

The Walker Brothers (9).

7

8

Something of a rock phenomenon, the ever-youthful Cliff Richard enjoys a wider audience than ever, despite being 43 years old and ceaselessly publicising his un-fashionable Christian beliefs. From his early rock days with the Shadows, to his own Middle of the Road TV variety shows, Cliff has gone full circle and returned to an uninhibited rock style.

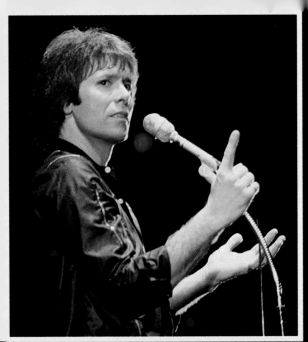

2
3

Conventional "nice guy" looks, a collar & tie and several hit singles, added up to the appeal of the young sixties crooner, **Billy J. Kramer** (2).

Ray Sawyer, an ex soul-singer from Chicksaw, Alabama, (wearing the eye-patch) teamed up with Dennis Locorriere, a New Jersey folk-singer, in the late sixties, to form the nucleus of the extraordinary American group **Dr. Hook** (1, 3, 4, 5, 6). Later joined by Billy Francis (keyboards), Rik Elswit (guitar), Rod Smarr (guitar and vocals), Jance Garfat (bass) and John Wolters (drums), Dr. Hook has proved successful on both sides of the Atlantic. Their success "Sylvia's Mother" was written by "Playboy" cartoonist/songwriter

5

6

8

Shel Silverstein, who discovered them playing in the New Jersey area. The late seventies were the best years for Dr. Hook, with memorable hits such as: "When You're in Love with a Beautiful Woman" and "Sexy Eyes." **The Box Tops** are shown (7) and **Paul Anka** (9).

Pictured here at the beginning of their hugely successful career, the six **Osmond** (8) brothers (part of an American Mormon family) later incorporated sister, Marie, in their act.

9
7

Marc Bolan (5, 6, 7 & 8). Born in 1947 in the East End of London, Mark Feld (as he then was) became a not unsuccessful male model whilst attempting to break into the pop scene as a songwriter. He later formed the "glam rock" band, Tyrannosaurus Rex, who had some success with Bolan's own compositions. He died tragically young (30) in September 1977, in a car driven by his girlfriend, American singer, Gloria Jones.

Another East End lad, **David Essex** (1, 2, 3, 4, & 9) had musical aspirations before being offered the lead role in the London stage production of "Godspell" in 1971. He followed that with a film part in the movie "That'll be the Day" and on the strength of the film's success, re-launched his own musical career, with very encouraging results: "Rock On" sold a million copies and Essex made a sequel movie, "Stardust" to cement his now superstar status. David Essex writes much of his own material and reaches both pop and rock audiences. His biggest success came in 1978 when he played the part of Che Guevara to Elaine Paige's Eva Peron, in the hit musical "Evita." For this performance David Essex won the Variety Club of Great Britain's Showbusiness Personality of the Year Award. A song from "Evita," "Oh, What a Circus" became a smash hit, as was the title track of his next film, "Silver Dream Racer."

The original 'cockney lad made good,' **Tommy Steele** (10) has been the inspiration for a whole generation of aspiring youngsters. His name was synonymous with rock 'n' roll in the early days and his talent, energy and charm are still a source of amazement to the world of showbusiness.

No prizes for guessing the identities of the four Liverpool lads on these pages. The names of Paul McCartney, the late John Lennon, George Harrison and Ringo Starr are etched forever on the minds of anyone old enough to have lived through the "Swinging Sixties."

Dubbed "Britain's Greatest Ambassadors" at this time, there is no question of the enduring talent of all the Beatles, both as songwriters and performers. Their first major hit single, "Please, Please Me" (1963) was quickly followed by other Beatles 'classics': "From Me to You," "She Loves You" and "I Want To Hold Your Hand," and Beatlemania was born. Hysteria, screams and mobbing followed the foursome wherever they went but they thrived on it, going on to make two highly

successful films, "A Hard Day's Night" and "Help," as well as a string of important singles and albums, all of which have had a tremendous effect in the shaping of contemporary music. Despite their unprecedented and lengthy success, the foursome could not remain together indefinitely; it was probably due to the fact that there was so much talent concentrated in one group that the inevitable split came. John Lennon (one half of the Lennon/McCartney songwriting duo) was becoming more politically aware and started making singles under the guise of "The Plastic Ono Band" with his Japanese-born wife, Yoko. McCartney was himself married to his American wife, Linda by this time and was the first to leave the original group.

BAGISM

LENNON FOREVER ano Peace On EARTH

In December 1980, the man who had tried to "Give Peace A Chance," met with his cruel and violent death. He was 40 years old. For many people John Lennon was much more than a musician, he was a spiritual leader, a guru. All over the world, people gathered to mourn together. In New York and in Liverpool, thousands gathered and as the sun set, the candles flickered and they said goodbye.

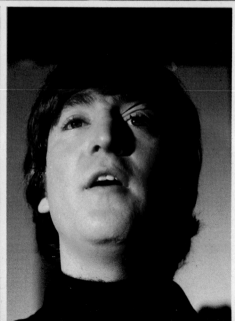

Duane Eddy (1). One of the earlier rock stars, remembered especially for his hit single "Guitar Man."

Little Richard (2). It is hard to believe that this heavily made-up and camply dressed personality took six years out of his music career to study theology! Remembered mostly for his early fifties gospel-style rock, Little Richard was in fact raised as a 7th Day Adventist and sang in church choirs as a boy. After completing his theological studies, Richard returned to the music scene in 1963 and broadened his repertoire as a soul and R&B-cum-rock singer. A controversial character much given to self-deification, Little Richard still has a loyal band of supporters, mainly in Britain.

Masters (along with Bad Manners) of "rock with laughs," **Madness** (3, 5) have an irrepressible quality which finds enthusiastic support in an exceptionally wide range of record

buyers. Originally known as the Invaders, this band came to light in Camden Town, North London, in 1978. Their first single, "The Prince," made No.16 in 1979 and success has followed in the US, France and Britain, with New Musical Express voting them Singles Artists of the Year in 1980, adding professional recognition to popularity. Bizarre, yet hilarious, Madness have brought a breath of fresh air and fun to the punk era!

Although American-born, (the fourth daughter of jazz bandleader Art Quatro) **Suzi Quatro** (4, 6 & 7) had her first recording contract in the U.K. where she still has her greatest following.

1

2 3

4 5

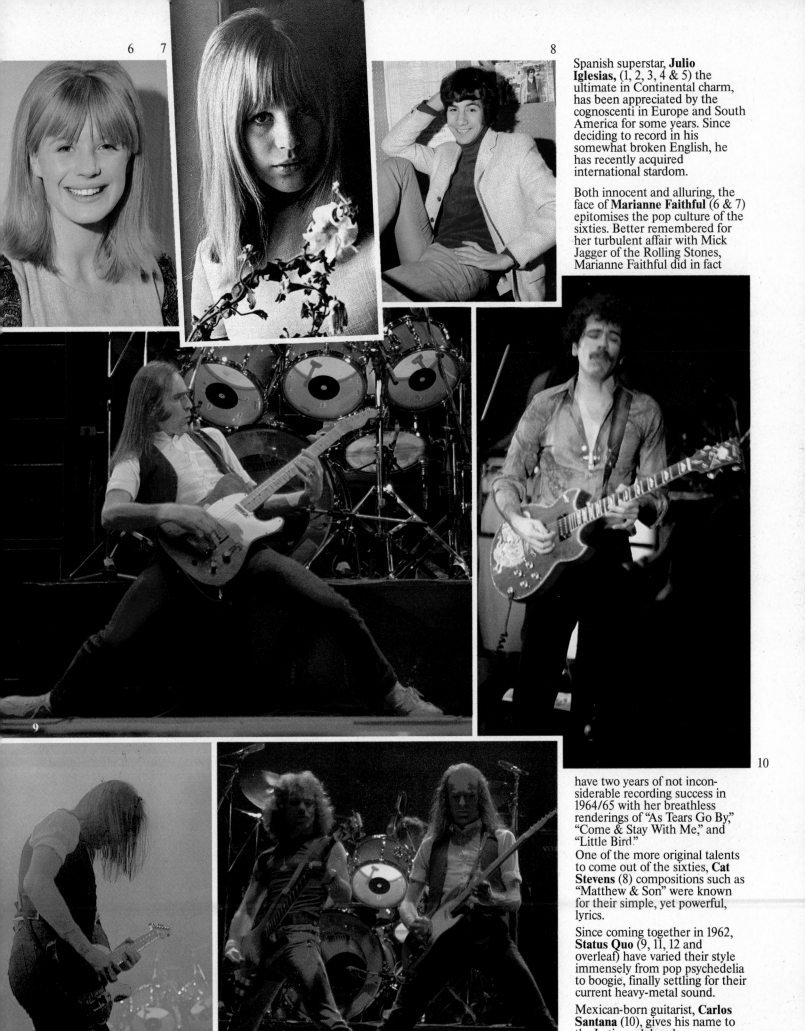

Spanish superstar, **Julio Iglesias,** (1, 2, 3, 4 & 5) the ultimate in Continental charm, has been appreciated by the cognoscenti in Europe and South America for some years. Since deciding to record in his somewhat broken English, he has recently acquired international stardom.

Both innocent and alluring, the face of **Marianne Faithful** (6 & 7) epitomises the pop culture of the sixties. Better remembered for her turbulent affair with Mick Jagger of the Rolling Stones, Marianne Faithful did in fact have two years of not inconsiderable recording success in 1964/65 with her breathless renderings of "As Tears Go By," "Come & Stay With Me," and "Little Bird."

One of the more original talents to come out of the sixties, **Cat Stevens** (8) compositions such as "Matthew & Son" were known for their simple, yet powerful, lyrics.

Since coming together in 1962, **Status Quo** (9, 11, 12 and overleaf) have varied their style immensely from pop psychedelia to boogie, finally settling for their current heavy-metal sound.

Mexican-born guitarist, **Carlos Santana** (10), gives his name to the Latin-rock band.

Born in England and raised in Australia, **Olivia Newton-John** (1, 2 and 3) is one of the most successful female acts in the United States. Her major breakthrough came with the world-wide box-office success of the film "Grease" which gave Olivia no less than three hit singles.

Simon & Garfunkel (4 & 5). It was the No.1 single, "The Sound of Silence" taken from their earlier debut album, that established the now legendary

Paul Simon and Art Garfunkel as major contributors to the contemporary folk-rock sound.

Together with his band, the Comets, **Bill Haley** (6, 9, 10 and 11) shook off his earlier Country & Western image and literally *created* Rock 'n' Roll in the early fifties, with numbers like "Rock Around the Clock" and "Shake Rattle & Roll."

With their clever harmonising the **Seekers** (7) were one of the more enduring groups to emerge from the folk-cult.

The Mojos (8): yet another of the many 'mod' pop groups of

6

7

the Beatles era who briefly leapt to stardom.

Born in the notorious Tiger Bay area of Cardiff, **Shirley Bassey** (12, 13) had to grasp stardom with both hands and she has become a legendary ballad-singing personality.

8

9

10

11

12   13

ABBA. This internationally acclaimed Swedish foursome first came to light when they won the Eurovision Song Contest in 1974, with their hit song, "Waterloo."

Although they had all been recording separately in Sweden for some years it was not until 1971 that they developed an act together and later in 1973 decided upon the name of Abba. From then on the four began to make shrewd commercial moves, not the least of which was to record all their material in English, obviously the key to international success!

Abba's music has since been criticised for its 'undiluted commercialism' and simplicity. As with so many highly professional performers in other fields, what may appear a simple matter in the hands of experts is in fact the result of great skill. Abba are extremely proficient in studio technology and it was not until 1977 that they finally agreed to make a significant number of live performances when they embarked upon their highly-successful world tour.

Abba's output is prolific and every single and album released has gone straight to the top of the charts. They have, in fact, outsold every group in recording history with the exception of the

Beatles, certainly justifying their commercial instincts.

Above (Left to Right)

Bjorn Ulvaeus – guitar/vocals

Agnetha Ulvaeus – vocals

Anni-Frid Lyngstad-Fredriksson – vocals

Benny Anderson – keyboard synthesiser/vocals

39

Dallas-born Marvin Lee Aday was nicknamed "Meatloaf" at the age of thirteen for obvious reasons! Despite two-year's treatment for paralysis of the right vocal chord, Meatloaf's performance is second to none for power and ferocity!

Tipped to become the pop phenomenon to take over the teeny-bopper market from the Bay City Rollers, **Adam Ant** (1) is moving away from his earlier 'punk pirate' style to appeal to a wider audience.

Legendary leader of the folk-protest movement, **Bob Dylan's** (2) importance to the development of rock music is rivalled only by that of the Beatles.

A popular boy and girl team, **"Dollar"** (3) broke away from Guys & Dolls to form their own singing duet.

A founder-member of the Animals, **Alan Price** (6) formed the Alan Price Set and later teamed up with **Georgie Fame** (5). Feeling that their combined talents were less than the sum of their individual ones, they too split up.

J. Geils Band (7). Thirteen years after they got together this hard-rock/blues band occupied the No.1 spot in both the US singles and album charts.

1

2

3

4

5 6

7

The songwriting team of Bacharach and David teamed up with Dionne Warwick to become one of the most successful hit-making partnerships of the sixties. Dionne has recently recorded under the guidance of Barry Manilow and the Bee Gees with renewed success.

The Rolling Stones. Two early shots showing the original line-up: (above) the late Brian Jones, Mick Jagger, Keith Richards, Bill Wyman and Charlie Watts.

Most controversial of all, lead singer Mick Jagger continues to amaze and excite audiences twenty years after the Rolling Stones exploded onto the pop scene with their wild music and equally wild lifestyles.

The Rolling Stones – Keith Richard (1, 4 & 5); Bill Wyman (2); and Mick Jagger (3).

The Animals (6, 10). Lead singer, Eric Burdon, a tough Geordie with a 'bad boy' reputation, lent this group their hard-rock image and the Animals were very successful during the early sixties.

Buddy Holly's first big hit "That'll Be the Day" was in fact originally credited to the Crickets as he formed the group and was their lead singer. After his death the Crickets continued to record and gig until 1973, making frequent appearances with solo artists like **Bobby Vee** (7, 9 & 11).

Eddie Cochran & **Gene Vincent** (8). These first-generation American rock 'n' rollers both enjoyed brief but memorable

careers during which they were both more popular in England than their native United States. Tragically, Cochran was killed in a car crash on the way to London Airport in 1960 after touring Britain with Gene Vincent. He was only 21. Gene Vincent continued to perform and record but alcoholism adversely affected his career and he too was dead by 1971.

Bobby Gentry (12). Popular Country & Western singer, most famed for her "Ode to Billy-Joe."

Barry White (13), pictured here with his female backing group 'Love Unlimited.' Barry White has commercialised soul music beyond recognition.

Ray Davies (1) and a vintage **Davies** and the **Kinks** (7).

Traffic (2).

Who can forget the influence the "Twist" had on the dancing habits of a whole generation, and its finest exponent, **Chubby Checker** (3)!

Peter Noone (4).

A regular performer with bandleader/trumpeter Dave Bartholemew, **Fats Domino's** (5) pounding up-tempo piano style made him a natural rock 'n' roller.

Donovan (6). In 1965 Britain's folk/flower-power composer achieved stardom when booked as resident on the TV rock programme "Ready Steady Go." In the same year his two self-composed singles "Catch The Wind" and "Colours" both made the British charts.

Given a lucky break by BBC TV documentary, "The Big Time" which took unknowns and gave them a chance, **Sheena Easton** (8, 9, 10 & 11) was shown nationwide in her attempts to get a recording contract. Her first single, "Modern Girl" was in the charts at No.8 at the same time as her second single, "Nine to Five," later to reach No.4.

8

9

10
11

Backed by American drummer Stewart Copeland and veteran of the British rock scene, Andy Summers, 'Sting' (real name Gordon Sumner) provides the 'girl appeal' for this highly original and successful rock band – Police.

1

2

3

4

5

Teddy Prendergrass (1, 2, 3 & 6) is a charismatic soul singer of the eighties, who puts a lot of emphasis on "feed-back" from his fans and audiences, whom he never fails to thank for the inspiration they give him.

Like so many groups formed in the sixties, **Manfred Mann** (4) had several years of pure pop success and then split up to pursue specialised musical careers. Manfred Mann's Earth Band sti'' features Mann on keyboards and Paul Jones has gone on to develop a career in song and drama.

Like the Beatles, **Gerry & The Pacemakers** (5) did much to put their home town, Liverpool, on the map, with numbers like "Ferry Across the Mersey" and "You'll Never Walk Alone," theme tune of Liverpool F.C.

7

Francis Vincent Zappa Jr. (7) was born of Sicilian-Greek parentage in Maryland in 1940. His career has been chequered, to say the least, including a spell in prison for making a sex tape. Zappa and The Mothers of Invention were noted for their weird and experimental music, with such album titles as: "Uncle Meat" and "Burnt Weenie Sandwich," to name but two. Since the late seventies Zappa has released a stream of albums that concentrate on more mellow sounds.

Elton John. "The Liberace of the Seventies" performing here in various types of head-gear, aimed at concealing the thinning hair beneath!

Elton John (1). Since the success of "Don't Go Breaking My Heart," his 1976 duet with Kiki Dee, Britain's Elton John has become an international superstar, renowned for his flamboyance and generosity.

The sound of Yorkshire 'heavy-metal' band **Saxon** (2 & 7), notable for big-scale shows, has been heard by audiences all over Europe, America and Japan.

Beach Boys (3). In 1961 five middle-class American boys created a completely new genre: Surf Music.

Rock 'n' roll's most frenetic pianist, **Jerry Lee Lewis** (4) was at the height of his career with the release of the classic rock number, "Great Balls of Fire" back in 1958.

Procul Harum (5 & 6). Their debut single "A Whiter Shade of Pale" (1967) shot to No.1 in a matter of a few weeks.

61

Phil Lynott of Thin Lizzie. Despite playing bass, Phil Lynott is the front-man for Thin Lizzie. An unusual and charismatic performer (Lynott is a black Irishman!) much of Thin Lizzie's hard-rock material has been written by him.

Britain's foremost exponent of "theatrical rock" **Bowie** (1, 2, 3, 4 & 6) was one of the shrewdest manipulators of the new visual era of the seventies.

West-Indian born songwriter turned performer, **Joan Armatrading** (5 & 10).

1

2

3

4

5

6

7

8

64

9

The five eldest sons of fifties guitarist Joe Jackson, the **Jackson 5** (7) were encouraged to develop their musical talent from an early age and became the best-selling Tamla Motown act.

Jimmy Hendrix (8); one of the "most important instrumentalists in the history of rock".

A persistent, if not wholly successful, performer, **Kiki Dee** (9) had a breakthrough in 1976 with "Don't Go Breaking My Heart".

Despite defections by two of

10

11

12

their number to religious cults, **Fleetwood Mac's** (11) popularity is growing in the U.S. as well as in Britain.

With hits "Somewhere" and "Maria," **P.J. Proby's** (12) main claim to fame was the fact that he regularly split his trousers while performing!

1

2   3

4

5

Jeff Lynne (guitar, vocals) and Bev Bevan (drums) are the nucleus of a strange collection of musicians, with backgrounds in either rock or classical music, though rarely both. Despite this unlikely combination of talents, **ELO** (1, 2, 3 and 4) are the perfect example of how not to put a foot wrong in show business; with their particular formula for orchestral rock they have produced a succession of hit singles and albums. ELO are regarded as a rock band of lasting quality with reserves of creative potential and enormous versatility.

In 1980 they collaborated with Olivia Newton-John on the title track of the rock musical "Xanadu."

Slade (5, 6 and 9). This energetic and gutsy foursome were first promoted as a skinhead band in the early seventies in an attempt to grab the adolescent market of the time. Although they now have a wider appeal, Slade have never lost their working-class, boot-stomping style!

In the early sixties **Adam Faith** (7 & 8) (really Acton-born Terence Nelhams) rivalled Cliff Richard as Britain's top teen idol. "What

6

7

Do You Want" reached No.1 in November 1959 and was quickly followed by other successes with titles such as "Poor Me" arousing the protective instincts of girl fans of the era. However, Faith's first love was acting and after several creditable film roles, he starred convincingly in the title role of the British TV series "Budgie," a portrayal of a small-time villain.

8

9

Rod Stewart's superstar status stemmed from his recording of the quintessential rock ballad "Maggie May," (a tale of a schoolboy's liaison with a hooker) and was reinforced by his No.1 success, "Sailin'" in 1979, a year of great personal upheaval for this self-styled idol of the "Tartan Hordes." His relationship with actress, Britt Ekland ended acrimoniously and the rebel rock-star married Alana Hamilton. Stewart is acknowledged as a first-class stage performer, generating a magic atmosphere at his sell-out gigs.

Both energetic and magnetic, the legendary Rod Stewart is seen here with Ron Wood.

Famous as much for his skin-tight leopard-skin pants as for his sandpaper voice, **Rod Stewart** is now enjoying world fame with all its trappings after nearly twenty years in the field of rock music. Stewart was born in North London in 1945, although his brothers were born in Scotland and he later found it convenient to gloss over his Sassenach origins when he adopted the Scottish tartan as a personal favour. Obsessed with football, Stewart and his original band, the Faces, would regularly kick footballs into the audience during a show and they were rewarded with the kind of worship normally reserved for soccer teams. In fact, Stewart signed as an apprentice with Brentford Football Club on leaving school, but became disillusioned with the harsh discipline and low wages and took to the road, where he learnt to play the banjo from English folksinger Wizz Jones.

Together with other rebel idols, such as the Who, Rod Stewart epitomises a certain gutsy anti-establishment attitude, always guaranteed to appeal to the younger generation, but he also has a large following among older rock fans, feeling the disillusionment of a society in recession.

Sandie Shaw (1) was the singing star of the sixties who came to be imitated by many for her habit of going barefoot!

Dave Clark Five (2, 8). All dressed identically here, this beat group of the sixties were unusual in having a drummer (Dave Clark) as their front man.

Bob Geldof (4, 6) is the lead singer of the Boom Town Rats, the band which emerged as a reckless anarchic force in Northern Ireland.

The unique country-rock sound of **Phil and Don Everly** (5) will remain one of the most enduring

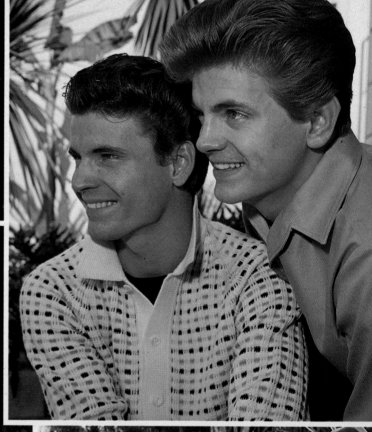

in rock music, as well as one of the most influential. Most popular in the fifties and sixties with such numbers as "Bye Bye Love," "All I Have To Do is Dream" and "Cathy's Clown," the brothers were the offspring of well-known U.S. country singers, Ike & Margaret Everly.

The Monkees (9). A manufactured group, put together in 1966 to perform in a TV series as America's answer to the Beatles, the group's music from the shows sold fantastically well! They made ten gold discs in two years, but success waned as quickly as it had been born.

3

Toyah Wilcox

Theatrical training has helped Toyah Wilcox to put together her extraordinarily visual act. She had numerous T.V., stage and film roles (such as Miranda in Derek Jarman's screen version of "The Tempest") before successfully breaking into the

1

2

A Durham miner's son, **Bryan Ferry** (1, 4, 6) was responsible for forming Roxy Music in 1970. The band seemed destined for success after the hugely favourable response to their early performances, but by the mid seventies Bryan Ferry had decided to project his cool rock style alone.

The Four Tops (2, 5) have retained the same line-up since

3

4

their formation in Detroit in 1954! They enjoyed huge success with Motown sounds such as "Reach Out I'll Be There" throughout the sixties and early seventies.

Despite apparently disappearing from the pop music scene when Beatlemania overturned the music-industry establishment, **Neil Sedaka's** (7, 8, 9 & 10) career as a singer/songwriter has been amazingly enduring. His first real hit was "Oh Carole," which he wrote for his then sweetheart Carole King, and many other pop classics followed. Sedaka made a highly successful comeback concert at the Albert Hall in 1971 when he promoted his album, "Emergence".

5

6

7

8

9

10

Making use of such stage props as electric chairs, boa-constrictors and gallows, Alice Cooper's act was the cause of much controversy among the record-buying public. Eventually slipping into self-parody, success has waned for Alice Cooper recently with the new wave moving away from grotesque theatricals.

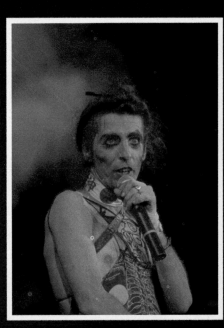

Unique in having a front-man (Ian Anderson) who played the flute, **Jethro Tull** (6 and facing page) took the musical "establishment" by surprise in 1968 when they shot to popularity. Their single "Living in The Past" is regarded as a classic contribution to rock.

Boney M (1, 3 & 7). "By The Rivers of Babylon" was soon on the lips of young and old alike, soon after its release by the glamorous quartet, Boney M. With their slick routines and glitzy clothes, Boney M became synonymous with the Glitter Rock genre.

Regarded by many as the

definitive heavy-metal rock combo, **Led Zeppelin** (2, 5) have spawned a host of imitators. They in fact emerged out of the dissolution of the Yardbirds back in 1968, for whom Jimmy Page played guitar.

The Moody Blues (4) had a sensational success with the No. 1 hit "Go Now" in 1965 which was followed by the legendary "Nights in White Satin" recorded in 1972.

Marty Wilde (8).

Undoubtedly, **Chuck Berry** (9) is one of the greatest contributors to rock 'n' roll and as an ex-convict, is one of its more notorious legends.

Paul McCartney, his wife Linda, and guitarist Denny Laine form the nucleus of McCartney's band, Wings.

Four faces of **Paul McCartney** (1, 2, 3, & 4), certainly the most commercially and artistically successful of all the ex-Beatles. Acknowledged as a brilliant songwriter (in partnership with the late John Lennon) Paul, with his band, Wings, shows no signs of abandoning his musical career despite his immense personal fortune.

2

3

1

4

Nazareth (5, 6, & 7). Dan McCafferty (vocals, pictured here), Pete Agnew (bass) and Daryl Sweet (drums) played together as a semi-professional band, the Shadettes. Joined by Manny Charlton (guitar) in 1969 they changed their name to Nazareth and acquired a reputation as a straight hard-rock band in their native Scotland. Since turning professional in 1971 Nazareth has gained a large following of fans impressed by the fact that the group throw everything into their stage act.

5

6

With lead singer Buster Bloodvessel, Bad Manners have been described as the 'musical equivalent to end-of-the-pier postcards'! In 1981 they had a major instrumental hit with their version of the "Can Can" complete with bald Buster in full female drag!

Acknowledged to be America's most successful entertainer, **Barry Manilow** is certainly one of the world's highest paid singers with a following of near Messianic fervour. Not since screaming girls mobbed the Beatles in the mid-sixties has any show-business personality received such a devoted following. Many fans, from tots to grandmothers, claim that the Brooklyn balladeer has provided them with a special inspiration to face life anew.

A great performer, **Barry Manilow** is also an accomplished songwriter and making use of his classical training he based his composition "Could It Be Magic" on Chopin's Prelude in C Minor. But it was the melodic single "Mandy" which first rocketed Barry to fame and started him on a seemingly unstoppable string of hit records, sell-out performances and world tours. There are some who find Barry Manilow's pure commercialism a

little unpalatable, but even his fiercest critics have had to admit that he has the combination of talent and perseverance that make a superstar out of a singer.

Mick Jagger (overleaf) of the Rolling Stones, still rocking on after twenty years in show business . . .

Featuring the Photography of David Wimsett.
First published in Great Britain 1983 by Colour Library International Ltd.
© 1983 Illustrations and Text: Colour Library International Ltd., 99 Park Avenue, New York, N.Y. 10016, U.S.A.
This edition is published by Crescent Books.
Distributed by Crown Publishers, Inc.
h g f e d c b a
Colour separations by FERCROM, Barcelona, Spain.
Display and text filmsetting by ACESETTERS LTD., Richmond, Surrey, England.
Printed and bound in Barcelona, Spain by JISA-RIEUSSET and EUROBINDER.
Library of Congress Catalog Card No. 82-70394
All rights reserved.
CRESCENT 1983

D.L. B-15.061-83